Brioche Knitting

Nancy Marchant

LEISURE ARTS, INC. • Maumelle, Arkansas

Meet the Designer

Nancy Marchant, aka the Queen of Brioche, was born and raised in Indiana where her mother taught her to knit. After graduating with a Master of Fine Arts degree in Textile Art, she moved to Amsterdam, the Netherlands.

It was in Amsterdam that she discovered the brioche stitch. She wrote the first article about this stitch in 1992. Since then, Nancy has written articles and designed for top magazines, published 5 books on brioche knitting, and traveled the world teaching the brioche love.

Thanks to Nancy, most of the top hand knitwear designers are now using the brioche stitch in their patterns.
For more of Nancy's designs, visit ravelry.com, her website www.briochestitch.com, Facebook, and Instagram.

Brioche Knitting

Brioche knitting creates a cushy reversible ribbed fabric. Because it is a ribbed stitch, it lays flat; making it perfect for shawls, scarves, and blankets. And it's fun.

Want to learn? Start by making a swatch. And practice the stitch until it feels comfortable; until you feel the rhythm of the stitch. You might have to start over several times and you will probably make mistakes. But teaching yourself how to brioche knit can be a rewarding experience. Something you'll want to share with your knitting friends.

The brioche stitch was first written about in the 1840's in England. Over the years, it has been known by many different names; Oriental Rib, Shawl Stitch, Patent Stitch, and Shaker Stitch to name a few. Today, brioche knitting is modern and uber trendy, essential for every fashion conscience knitter to know.

Let's knit some brioche!

Contents

Brioche Knitting Tips

Brioche knitting involves a set of two stitches. One stitch is worked and the other is slipped. The slipped stitch in brioche knitting is abbreviated as a "sl1yo". In brioche knitting, instead of carrying the working yarn in front or in back of the slipped stitch, you bring the yarn over the stitch and over the needle, giving the stitch a little shawl over its shoulders. It is this sl1yo that makes brioche, brioche. In the following row, this shawled stitch will be either brioche knit (brk) or brioche purled (brp).

This stitch with its yarn over is considered ONE stitch. The yarn over is not counted separately. When you count 4 stitches hanging on your needle, you will actually have 6 loops of yarn.

Brioche knitting uses more yarn; up to twice as much.

For brioche knitting, it is best to avoid slippery yarns. Slippery yarns have a tendency to 'grow' lengthwise. If you want cushiness and to help control the 'give', it can be advisable to go down in needle size.

Note that a normal brioche gauge will have fewer stitches but more rows than conventional knitting.

CASTING ON AND BINDING OFF

Given the elasticity of brioche, you should cast on and bind off loose instead of tight. Long-Tail Cast On and a standard knitted bind off works fine. I also suggest the Stem Stitch Bind Off which matches the Long Tail Cast On. You can read more about binding off on pages 58 and 59.

After casting on, it takes 8 to 10 worked rows before a pattern can be recognized.

COUNTING ROWS

Because every other stitch is slipped, you have to work each row twice in order to have worked all of the stitches in that row. Two worked rows = one counted row. When you see the gauge for a project, it will often say "XX <u>counted</u> rows". That means that you have worked back and forth XX times.

This sample measures 22 "counted" rows for 4 inches. This means that 22 rows have also been worked back and forth.

CORRECTING MISTAKES

I have been "brioching" for years and still find the stitch difficult to read. If you make a mistake in the middle of a row, don't tear out the entire row at once; instead, work back one stitch at a time. If the mistake lies a few rows down, rip out all the rows until one row above the mistake. From there, rip out stitch by stitch. You will be picking up normal-looking stitches as well as stitches with yarn overs. Pick up the stitches onto a smaller needle. This will make the stitches easier to pick up. You can work off this needle onto your original needle for your next row.

Please see page 57 on how to correct a dropped yarn over.

Brioche Knitting Abbreviations and Terminology

Before we start, let's break down the terminology. If you're learning brioche knitting for the first time, some of these terms may be new to you.

brk (brioche knit) = knit the stitch (that was slipped in the previous row) together with its yarn over.

brp (brioche purl) = purl the stitch (that was slipped in the previous row) together with its yarn over.

The **sl1yo** is the action that creates the shawled stitch. This action works differently for a brk row than for a brp row, but one manipulation remains standard – that the working yarn must always be in front before slipping the stitch. On a brp row the working yarn is in place before slipping the stitch but in a bark row you need to first bring the yarn to the front and then slip the stitch. This worked stitch with its yarn over shawl is considered one stitch.

sl1yo following a k or brk st = bring the working yarn under the needle to the front of the work, slip the next stitch purlwise, then bring the yarn over the needle (and over the slipped stitch) to the back, in position to work the following knit or brioche knit stitch.

sl1yo following a p or brp st = the working yarn is already in front, slip the next stitch purlwise, then bring the yarn over the needle (and over the slipped stitch), then back to the front under the needle, into position to work the following purl or brioche purl stitch.

brLsl dec (2-stitch decrease that slants to the left, involves 3 sts) = slip the first stitch kwise, brk the following two stitches together, pass the slipped stitch over.

Make a swatch - Working a sl1yo, brk1

Using the needle size recommended for the yarn and the Long-Tail Cast On, CO 18 stitches (or any even number of stitches).

Set-Up Row: sl1 wyib, *k1, sl1yo; rep from * to last st, k1.

Brioche Row 1: sl1 wyib (pull yarn tight), *brk1, sl1yo; rep from * to last st, k1.

Repeat **Brioche Row 1** until you feel comfortable with the stitch. BO.

If your swatch feels too loose, go down a needle size or two.

SET-UP ROW - you will work this row once.

Set-Up Row: *after slipping the edge stitch, be sure and pull the yarn tight.*

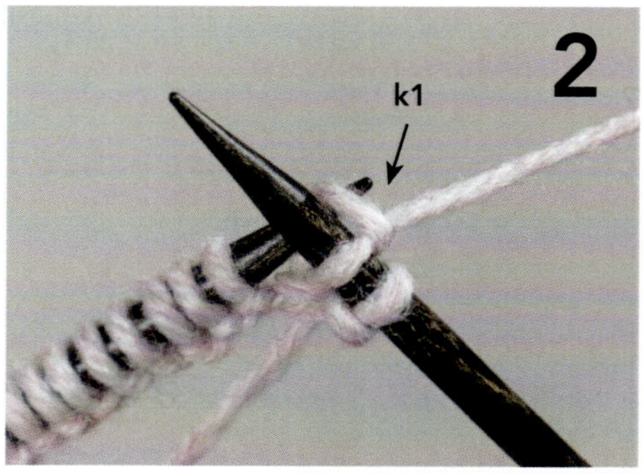

k1,

**sl1yo = bring the working yarn to the front by going under the right hand needle, slip the following stitch purlwise, carry the working yarn over the slipped stitch, and at the same time begin working a k1...*

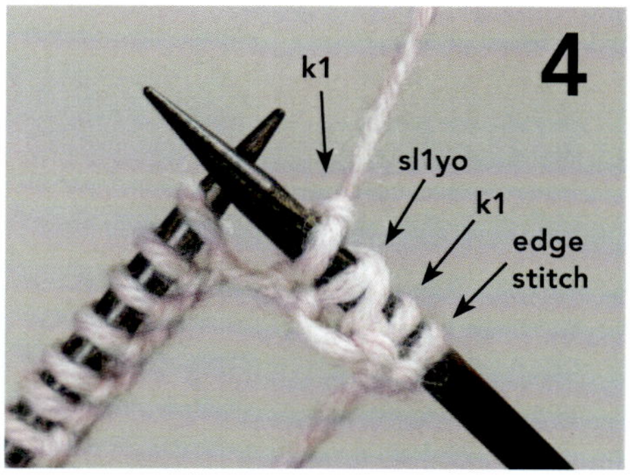

*... k1, repeat from *.*

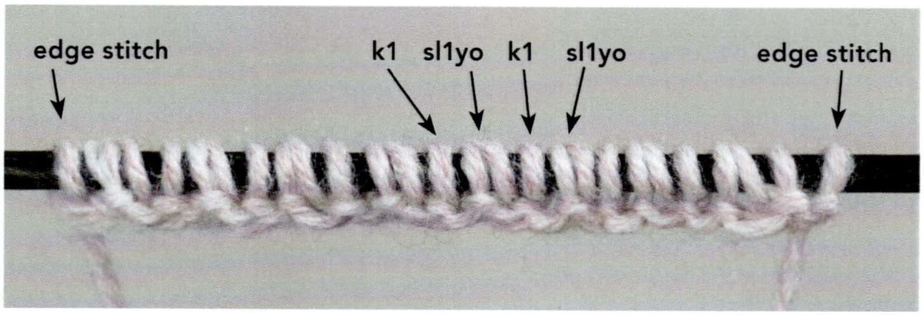

This is a completed Set-Up Row.
Note that every other stitch has a shawl (those are the sl1yo stitches).

BRIOCHE ROW 1 - you will repeat this row.

Row 1: *slip the edge stitch purlwise holding the working yarn to the back.*

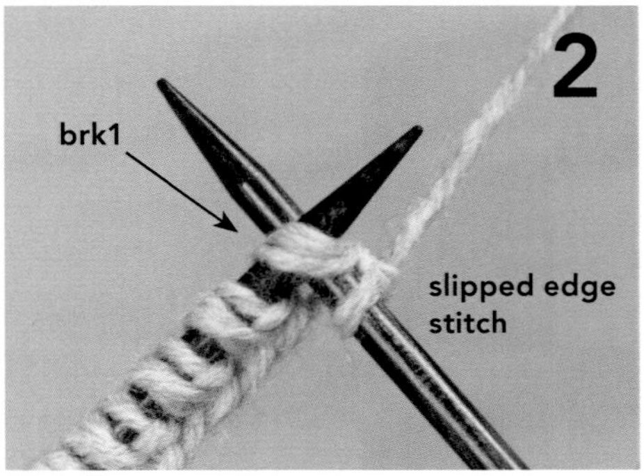

brk1 = knit the stitch and its yarn over together,

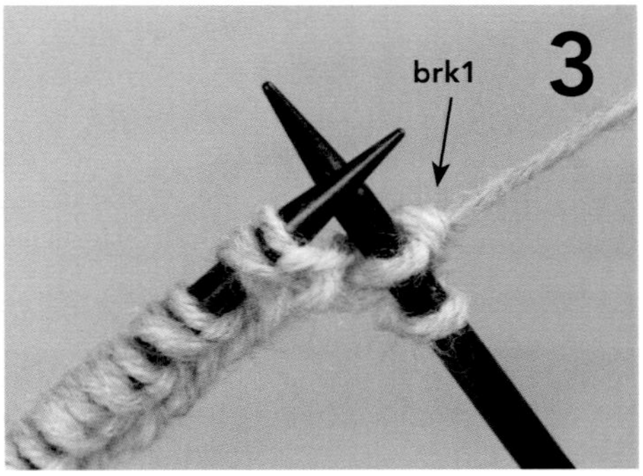

**sl1yo = bring the working yarn to the front by going under the right hand needle,*

slip the following stitch purlwise and at the same time begin working a brk1,

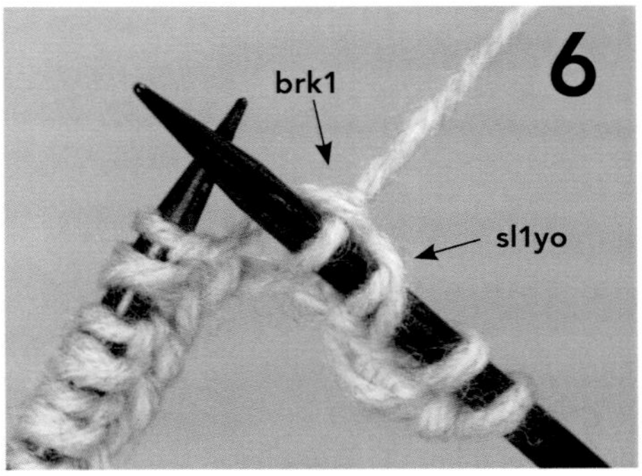

*carry the working yarn over the slipped stitch, brk1; repeat from * to last 2 stitches. End with sl1yo, k1 (the edge stitch).*

This is a completed Brioche Row 1.
Repeat Brioche Row 1 until desired length. To bind off, please *see pages 58 an 59.*

Working a sl1yo, brp1

Brioche purled fabric looks exactly like brioche knitted fabric. When working with brp stitches, the yarn is already in the front for the sl1yo. After slipping the stitch, carry the yarn over the needle and slipped stitch, then back to the front to work the following brp stitch.

The visuals show a sample using a single selvedge edge stitch.

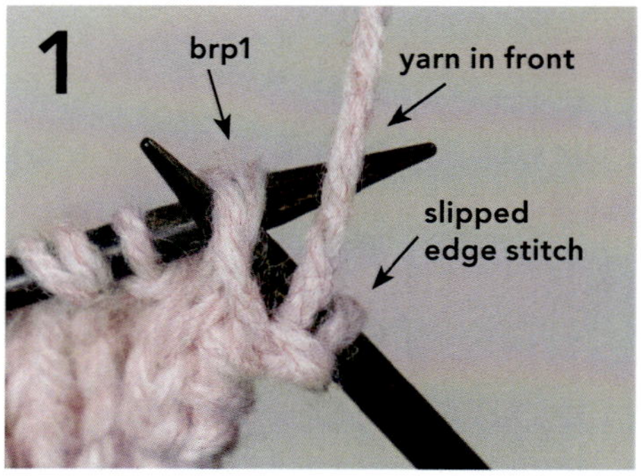

After slipping the edge stitch with the yarn held to the back, bring the yarn to the front and...

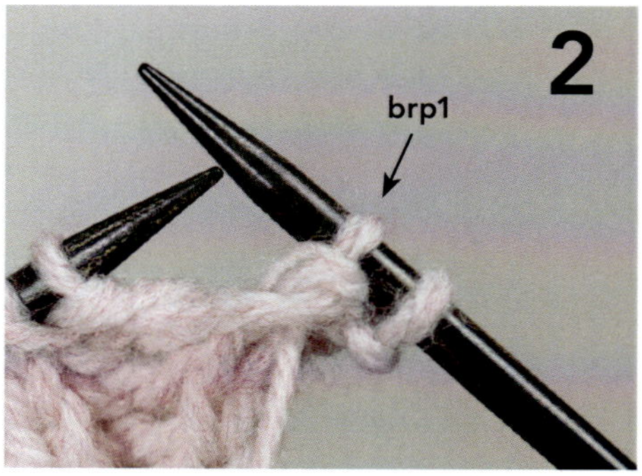

... brp1 = purl the stitch together with its yarn over,

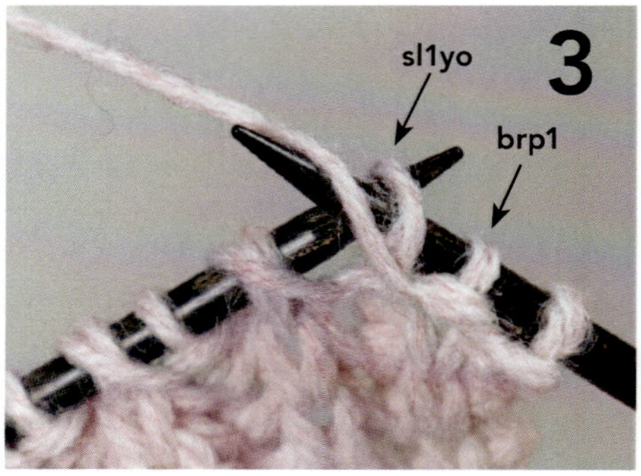

**sl1yo = the yarn is hanging in front, sl1 purlwise...*

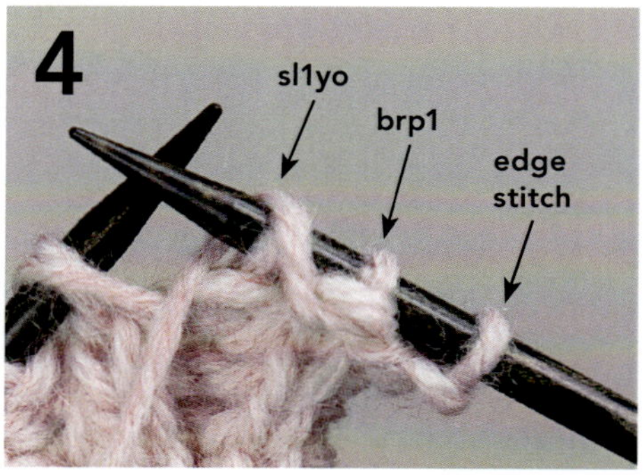

... carry the yarn over the needle and slipped stitch then back to the front, ...

... work the following brp1.

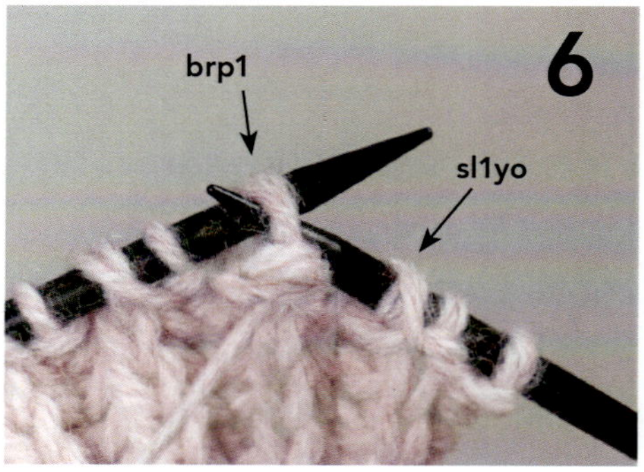

*brp = purl the following stitch together with its yarn over. Repeat from * to last 2 stitches. End with sl1yo, k1*

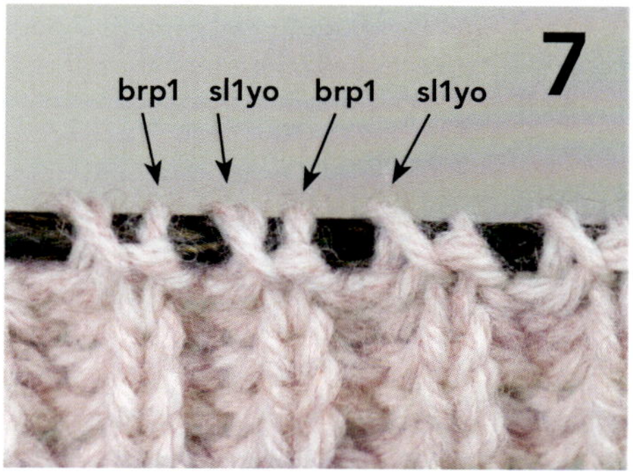

This is a completed brp row. Notice the brp stitch on top of a brk column.

Two-Color Brioche in the Round

Two rounds are worked for every round that appears on the face of the fabric. Be sure and hang a marker between the last stitch and first stitch of the round.

A brioche knit round is worked with the main color (MC), then a brioche purl round is worked with the contrast color (CC).

Don't cross your yarns when changing colors at the beginning of a round. At the end of an MC brioche knit round, your last stitch will be a sl1yo (Figure 2). Drop the MC yarn to the front after creating the sl1yo. Pick up the CC that is laying underneath (don't cross yarns) and work next round as a brioche purl, starting with a sl1yo. That's right, the MC round ends with a sl1yo and the CC round begins with a sl1yo.

At the end of a CC brioche purl round, the last stitch is a brp1. Maintain the MC yarn over to work this last brp stitch. Drop CC yarn to the front after working the stitch, then pick up MC (don't cross yarns) and take it to the back to work a brioche knit round, starting with a brk1. You end a CC round with a brp1 and begin the MC round with a brk1 (Figure 5).

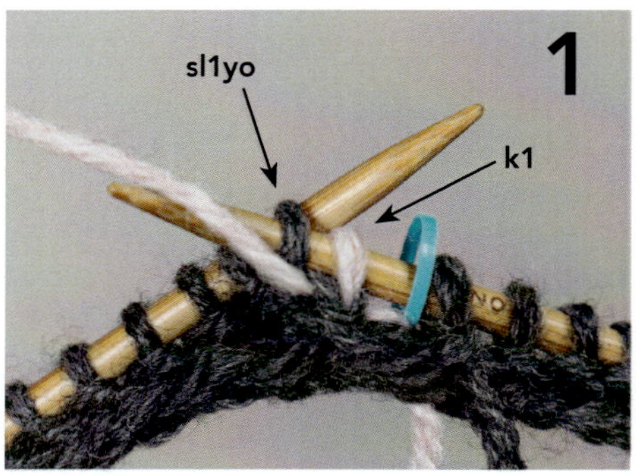

The visual shows 2 rows of garter stitch worked in CC.
***Set-Up Round,** with MC: *k1, sl1yo; rep from *.*

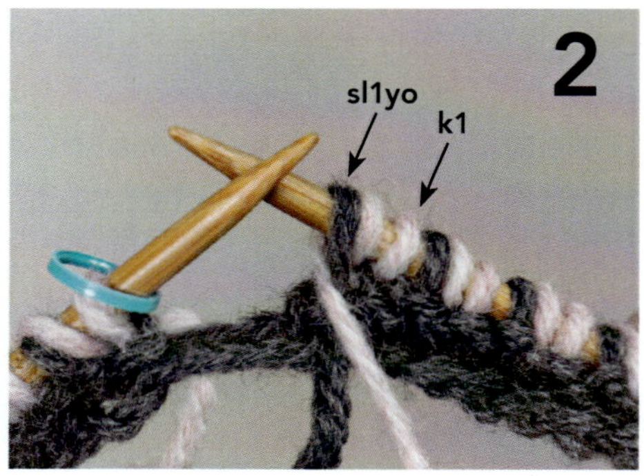

*At the **end of a MC round**, the last stitch is a sl1yo. Work the sl1yo and hang the MC yarn to the front.*

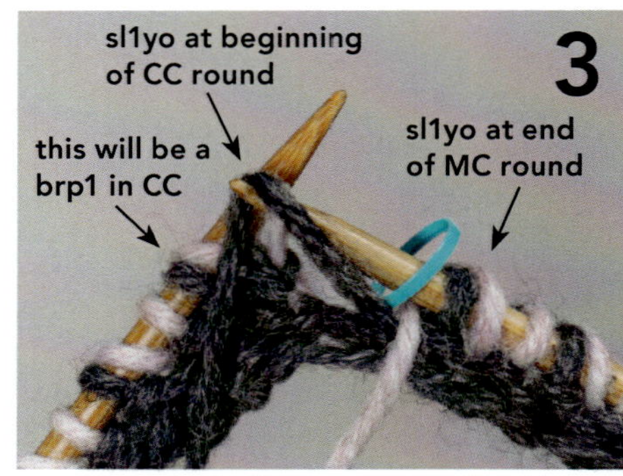

***Beginning of CC Round**: pick up CC from under the hanging MC yarn and work *sl1yo, brp1; rep from *.*

*The **CC round ends** with a brp1. Drop the CC yarn in the front, pick up the MC yarn, which now hangs on top of the just worked CC yarn,*

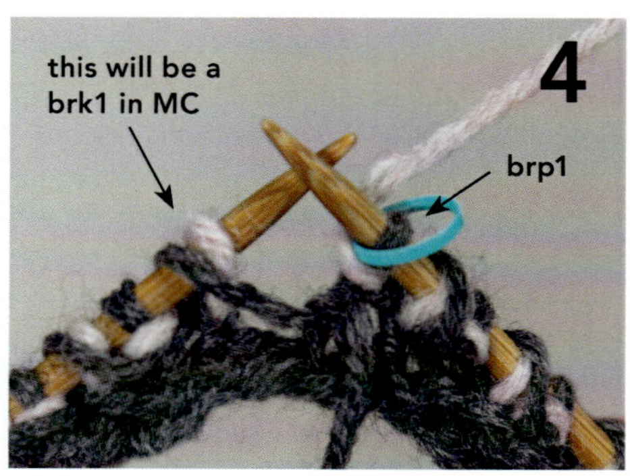

take MC to the back, slip marker, and begin MC round.

***MC Round**: *brk1, sl1yo; rep from *.*
Then work a CC round.
Repeat MC round, CC round.

Making a Left Slant Decrease-brLsl dec

brLsl dec (2-stitch decrease that slants to the left, involves 3 sts) = slip the first stitch **knitwise**, brk the following two stitches together, pass the slipped stitch over.

To maintain the integrity of the brioche stitch, decreases should be worked in pairs of stitches.

When you are instructed to slip a stitch, remember that the stitch and its yarn over are considered one stitch so be sure and slip the stitch together with its yarn over.

In the visuals, the first column of the round is shown with a pink marker.

Slip the first stitch (with its yarn over) KNITWISE...

... brk the following two stitches together, ...

... pass the slipped stitch over.

Finished 2 stitch decrease.

Classic Brioche Scarf

SHOPPING LIST

YARN

(Medium Weight)
[3.5 ounces, 186 yards
(100 grams, 170 meters) per skein]:
☐ 4 skeins

KNITTING NEEDLES

Straight
☐ Size 8 (5 mm) or size needed for gauge

FINISHED SIZE

9"wide x 74" long (23 cm x 188 cm)

GAUGE

In brioche stitch, 17 sts and 21 counted rows = 4" (10 cm)

TECHNIQUES USED

• brk1, sl1yo *(See pages 8 and 9)*

EASY

PATTERN NOTES

The first edge stitch of every row is a "sl1 wyib". After slipping this stitch, be sure and pull the yarn tight.

INSTRUCTIONS

CO 38 sts (an even number of stitches).

Set-Up Row: sl1 wyib, *k1, sl1yo; rep from * to last st, k1.

Row 1: sl1 wyib (pull yarn tight), *brk1, sl1yo; rep from * to last st, k1.

Repeat **Row 1** until piece measures 74" (188 cm) long or to desired length.

Bind off. Weave in ends. Lightly steam block if the edges are flared.

DESIGNER TIPS

This pattern could easily be worked in stripes of different colors, like collegiate fan club colors.

Bulky Brioche Scarf

SHOPPING LIST

YARN

(Super Bulky Weight) 6 SUPER BULKY
[10 ounces, 174 yards
(283 grams, 159 meters) per skein]:
☐ 2 skeins

KNITTING NEEDLES

Straight
☐ Size 13 (9 mm) or size needed for gauge

FINISHED SIZE

8"wide x 86" long (20 cm x 218.5 cm)

GAUGE

In brioche stitch, 9 sts and 10 counted rows = 4" (10 cm)

TECHNIQUES USED

- brk1, sl1yo *(See pages 8 and 9)*

EASY

DESIGNER TIP

If you would prefer a cowl, you could knit a shorter scarf and sew the CO and BO together.

PATTERN NOTES

The first edge stitch of every row is a "sl1 wyib". After slipping this stitch, be sure and pull the yarn tight.

INSTRUCTIONS

CO 18 sts (an even number of stitches).

Set-Up Row: sl1 wyib, *k1, sl1yo; rep from * to last st, k1.

Row 1: sl1 wyib (pull yarn tight), *brk1, sl1yo; rep from * to last st, k1.

Repeat **Row 1** until piece measures 86" (218.5 cm) long or to desired length.

Bind off. Weave in ends. Lightly steam block if the edges are flared.

Headband

SHOPPING LIST

YARN
(Medium Weight) 4 MEDIUM
[1.75 ounces, 120 yards
(50 grams, 110 meters) per skein]:

- ☐ 1 skein

KNITTING NEEDLES
Straight

- ☐ Size 6 (4 mm) or size needed for gauge

ADDITIONAL SUPPLIES
- ☐ Stitch marker
- ☐ Tapestry needle

FINISHED SIZE
3½" wide x 19" circumference (9 cm x 48.5 cm)

GAUGE
In brioche stitch, 18 sts = 3½" (9 cm) and
22 counted rows = 4" (10 cm)

TECHNIQUES USED
- brk1, sl1yo *(See pages 8 and 9)*

EASY

PATTERN NOTES

Headband is worked in one piece and seamed at the back.

Hang a marker on the right side of the work.

The first edge stitch of every row is a "sl1 wyib". After slipping this stitch, be sure and pull the yarn tight.

You want to make the headband tighter rather than looser; it will stretch.

INSTRUCTIONS

CO 18 sts (an even number of stitches).

RIBBING

Ribbing Row 1: *p1, k1; repeat from *.

Rep **Ribbing Row 1**, 11 more times.

HEAD WRAP IN BRIOCHE

Set-Up Row: sl1 wyib, *k1, sl1yo; rep from * to last st, k1.

Brioche Row 1: sl1 wyib (pull yarn tight), *brk1, sl1yo; rep from * to last st, k1.

Repeat **Brioche Row 1** until piece measures 17½"/44cm, ending with a WS row.

RIBBING

Next Row: *p1, brk1; rep from * to last 2 sts, p1, k1.

Ribbing Row 1: *p1, k1; repeat from *.

Rep **Ribbing Row 1**, 10 more times.

Bind off. When bind off is finished, cut the yarn 4 times longer than the width of the edge and use it to sew the BO/CO together. Sew CO edge to BO edge. Weave in ends. Lightly steam block if the edges are flared.

DESIGNER TIPS

You could make the ribbing section longer so that you could tie the two ends of the headband in the back.

You might like to add color by making the ribbing a different color than the head wrap.

Brioche Garter Block Scarf

SHOPPING LIST

YARN
(Medium Weight) 4 MEDIUM
[3.5 ounces, 210 yards
(100 grams, 192 meters) per skein]:
☐ 3 skeins

KNITTING NEEDLES
Straight
☐ Size 7 (4.5 mm) or size needed for gauge

ADDITIONAL SUPPLIES
☐ Stitch markers - 4

FINISHED SIZE
8" wide x 67" long (20 cm x 170 cm)

GAUGE
In Brioche Garter Block pattern, one repeat (14 sts) = 3" (7.5 cm) and 12 counted rows = 2.5" (6.25 cm)

TECHNIQUES USED
- brk1, sl1yo *(See pages 8 and 9)*

INTERMEDIATE

PATTERN NOTES

Hang a marker on the right side (RS) of the work.

Hang markers between each pattern. "pm" (place marker) is indicated in the first row of the pattern. In the following rows, slip markers when you come to them.

The first edge stitch of every row is a "sl1 wyib". After slipping this stitch, be sure and pull the yarn tight.

INSTRUCTIONS

CO 37 sts.

Set-Up Row 1 RS: sl1 wyib, *(k1, sl1yo) 3 times, k1, pm, k7, pm; rep from * to last 8 sts, (k1, sl1yo) 3 times, k2.

Set-Up Row 1 WS: sl1 wyib, *(sl1yo, brk1) 3 times, sl1yo, k7; rep from * to last 8 sts, (sl1yo, brk1) 3 times, sl1yo, k1.

Row 2 RS: sl1 wyib, *(brk1, sl1yo) 3 times, brk1, k7; rep from * to last 8 sts, (brk1, sl1yo) 3 times, brk1, k1 .

Row 2 WS: sl1 wyib, *(sl1yo, brk1) 3 times, sl1yo, k7; rep from * to last 8 sts, (sl1yo, brk1) 3 times, sl1yo, k1.

Repeat **Rows 2 RS and WS** 4 more times.

Set-Up Row 7 RS: sl1 wyib, *(brk1, k1) 3 times, brk1, (k1, sl1yo) 3 times, k1; rep from * to last 8 sts, (brk1, k1) 4 times.

Set-Up Row 7 WS: sl1 wyib, *k7, (sl1yo, brk1) 3 times, sl1yo; rep from * to last 8 sts, k8.

Row 8 RS: sl1 wyib, *k7, (brk1, sl1yo) 3 times, brk1; rep from * to last 8 sts, k8.

Row 8 WS: sl1 wyib, *k7, (sl1yo, brk1) 3 times, sl1yo; rep from * to last 8 sts, k8.

Repeat **Rows 8 RS and WS** 4 more times.

Set-Up Row 13 RS: sl1 wyib, *(k1, sl1yo) 3 times, k1, (brk1, k1) 3 times, brk1; rep from * to last 8 sts, (k1, sl1yo) 3 times, brk1, k1 .

Set-Up Row 13 WS: sl1 wyib, *(sl1yo, brk1) 3 times, sl1yo, k7; rep from * to last 8 sts, (sl1yo, brk1) 3 times, sl1yo, k1.

Row 14 RS: sl1 wyib, *(brk1, sl1yo) 3 times, brk1, k7; rep from * to last 8 sts, (brk1, sl1yo) 3 times, brk1, k1.

Row 14 WS: sl1 wyib, *(sl1yo, brk1) 3 times, sl1yo, k7; rep from * to last 8 sts, (sl1yo, brk1) 3 times, sl1yo, k1.

Repeat **Rows 14 RS and WS** 4 more times.

Rep from **Set-Up Row 7 RS** until desire length.

Bind off. Weave in ends.

DESIGNER TIP

This pattern would work well as a shawl or blanket. Just add multiples of 14 stitches to make it wider.

Brioche Cowlette

SHOPPING LIST

YARN

6 SUPER BULKY

(Super Bulky Weight)
[3.5 ounces, 89 yards
(100 grams, 81 meters) per skein]:

☐ 1 skein makes one scarf

KNITTING NEEDLES

Straight

☐ Size 11 (8 mm) or size needed for gauge

ADDITIONAL SUPPLIES

☐ Stitch marker

☐ Decorative button(s)

FINISHED SIZE

5½" wide x 27-29" long (14 cm x 68.5-73.5 cm)
(the length varies between the different yarn colorways)

GAUGE

In brioche stitch, 9 sts and 12 counted rows = 4" (10cm)

TECHNIQUES USED

- brk1, sl1yo *(See pages 8 and 9)*

EASY

PATTERN NOTES

Hang a marker on the right side of the work.

This cowl has a two-stitch i-cord edging.

INSTRUCTIONS

CO 15 sts (an uneven number of stitches).

Set-Up Row WS: wyif, sl2, yb, *k1, sl1yo; rep from * to last 3 sts, k1, yf, sl2.

Row 1 RS: Pull yarn tight, k2, *sl1yo, brk1; rep from * to last 3 sts, sl1yo, k2.

Row 1 WS: wyif, sl2, yb (pull yarn tight), *brk1, sl1yo; rep from * to last 3 sts, brk1, yf, sl2.

Repeat **Row 1 RS and WS** until desired length ending with a WS row.

Bind off. Weave in ends. Close the cowl by sewing buttons through both layers or sewing the edges together.

DESIGNER TIPS

This is a very simple scarf with a lot of design possibilities.

You might like to use a shawl pin instead of a button.

You could sew the CO and BO together making it a circular cowl or slightly overlap the CO and BO edge and finish with 3 buttons.

Keep it plain. Overlap the edges, as shown for the Autumn cowl, but eliminate the buttoms and simply sew down the outside edges of the overlapping "V".

Poncho

SHOPPING LIST

YARN

(Medium Weight) 4 MEDIUM

[3 ounces, 197 yards

(85 grams, 180 meters) per skein]:

- ☐ Beige - 1 skein
- ☐ Blush Pink - 1 skein
- ☐ Rose Pink - 1 skein
- ☐ Light Grey - 1 skein
- ☐ Dark Grey - 1 skein

KNITTING NEEDLES

Straight

- ☐ Size 7 (4.5 mm) or size needed for gauge

ADDITIONAL SUPPLIES

- ☐ Tapestry needle or crochet hook to sew seams

FINISHED SIZE OF EACH PIECE

16" wide x 24" long (41.5 cm x 61 cm)

GAUGE

In brioche stitch, 15.5 sts and 20 counted rows = 4" (10 cm)

TECHNIQUES USED

- brk1, sl1yo *(See pages 8 and 9)*

EASY

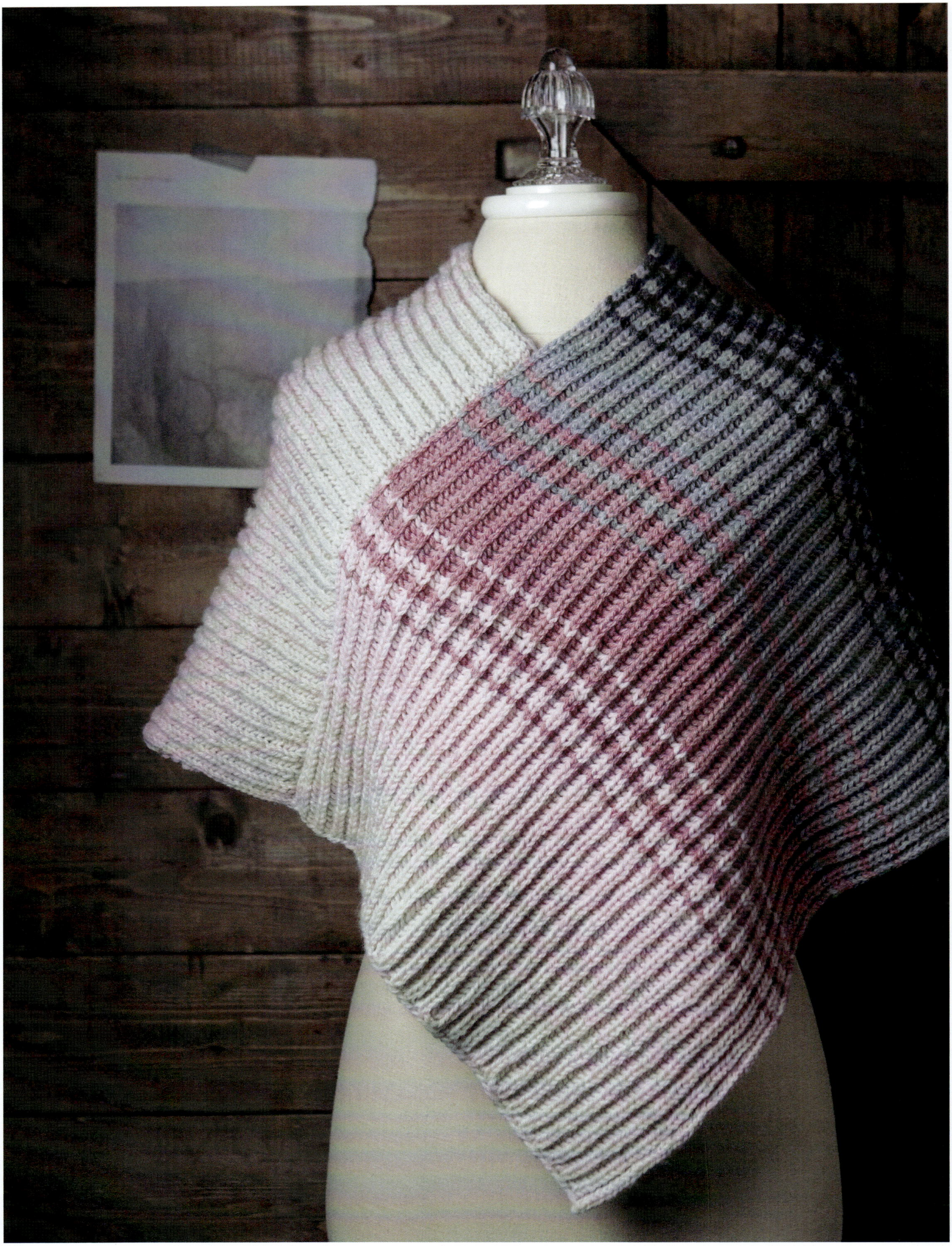

PATTERN NOTES

Leave long tails at the cast on and bind off to use for sewing the pieces together.

Hang a marker on the right side of the work.

When you are told to work 1 row of a color that means knitting a RS and a WS row of that color. Remember, two worked rows = one counted row.

All stripes begin on the RS.

This poncho has a two-stitch i-cord edging.

Don't cut the yarns until you are done with the entire striping of the color; carry the yarns up inside the i-cord edging.

INSTRUCTIONS (MAKE 2)

With Beige, CO 63 sts.

Set-Up Row WS: wyif, sl2, yb, *k1, sl1yo; rep from * to last 3 sts, k1, yf, sl2.

Row 1 RS: Pull yarn tight, k2, *sl1yo, brk1; rep from * to last 3 sts, sl1yo, k2.

Row 1 WS: wyif, sl2, yb (pull yarn tight), *brk1, sl1yo; rep from * to last 3 sts, brk1, yf, sl2.

Following the STRIPE SEQUENCE CHART, repeat **Row 1 RS and WS.**

Bind off. Weave in ends at each color change. Lightly steam block the two pieces.

Sew bottom edge B to side edge A and top edge A to side edge B, leaving an 8" (20.5 cm) neck opening. See Figure 1 on the following page.

STRIPE SEQUENCE CHART

(back and forth = 1 row)

Beige	12 rows
Blush Pink	1 row
Beige	3 rows
Blush Pink	2 rows
Beige	2 rows
Blush Pink	3 rows
Beige	1 row
Blush Pink	12 rows
Rose Pink	1 row
Blush Pink	3 rows
Rose Pink	2 rows
Blush Pink	2 rows
Rose Pink	3 rows
Blush Pink	1 row
Rose Pink	12 rows
Light Grey	1 row
Rose Pink	3 rows
Light Grey	2 rows
Rose Pink	2 rows
Light Grey	3 rows
Rose Pink	1 row
Light Grey	12 rows
Dark Grey	1 row
Light Grey	3 rows
Dark Grey	2 rows
Light Grey	2 rows
Dark Grey	3 rows
Light Grey	1 row
Dark Grey	12 rows
Beige	1 row
Dark Grey	3 rows
Beige	2 rows
Dark Grey	2 rows
Beige	3 rows
Dark Grey	1 row

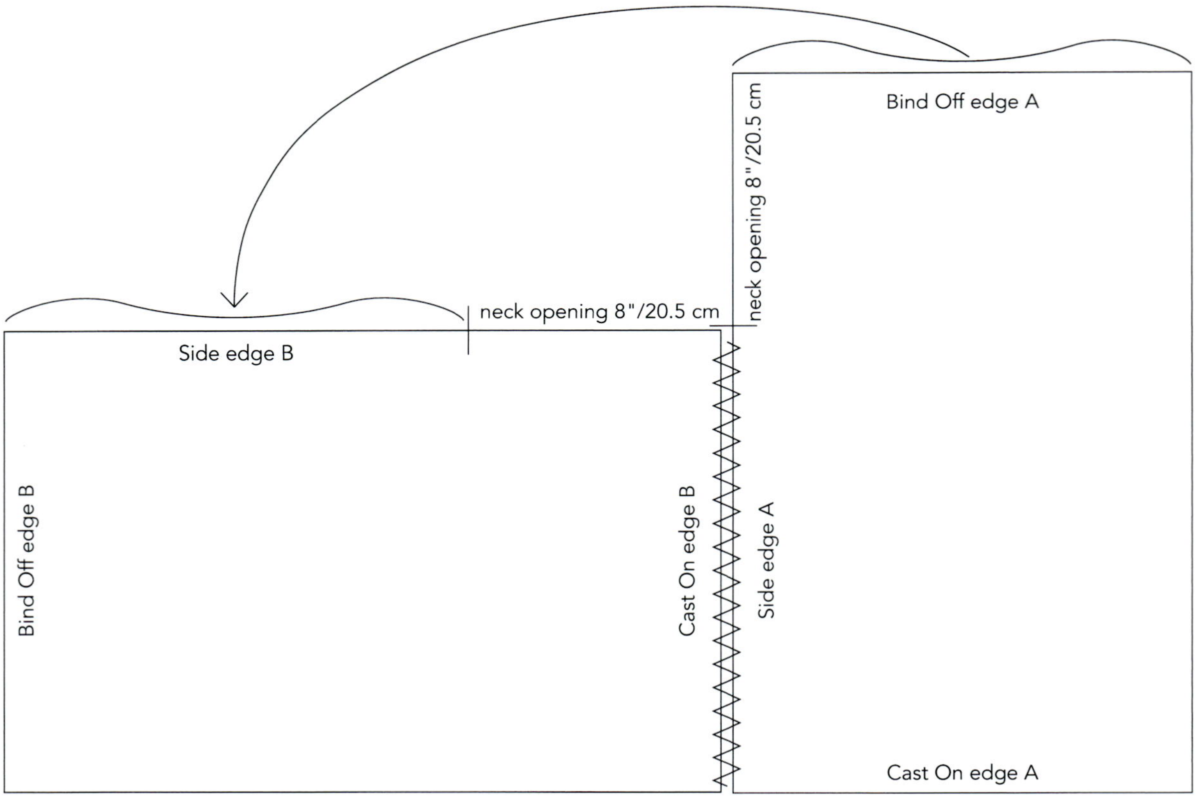
Bind Off edge A
neck opening 8"/20.5 cm
neck opening 8"/20.5 cm
Side edge B
Bind Off edge B
Cast On edge B
Side edge A
Cast On edge A

Figure 1

DESIGNER TIPS

This poncho would also look good made in only two colors.

Change the striping. Maybe make all the stripes 12 counted rows high.

You could trend it up a bit by adding a tassel at the bottom point or fringe at the bottom edges.

Keyhole Scarf

SHOPPING LIST

YARN

(Bulky Weight) 5 BULKY
[5.3 ounces, 312 yards
(150 grams, 285 meters) per skein]:

- [ ] 1 skein will make 2 scarves

KNITTING NEEDLES

Straight

- [ ] Size 7 (4.5 mm) or size needed for gauge

Two 16" (40.5 cm) Circulars

- [ ] Size 5 (3.75 mm) or smaller; these will only be used to hold stitches when working the keyhole.

ADDITIONAL SUPPLIES

- [ ] Stitch marker

FINISHED SIZE

4¾" wide x 30" long (12 cm x 76 cm)

GAUGE

In brioche stitch, 15 sts and 20 counted rows = 4" (10 cm)

TECHNIQUES USED

- brk1, sl1yo *(See pages 8 and 9)*
- brp1, sl1yo *(See page 10)*

INTERMEDIATE

PATTERN NOTES

The tails of this scarf are worked in syncopated brioche. Syncopated brioche is where you switch your brioche knits for brioche purls and vice versa. This causes the brioche knit columns to recede into a purl ditch and the purl columns to come forward into knit columns.

This scarf starts with knitting the first tail. The first tail is designed with 8 rows of brioche knit followed by 8 rows of brioche purl. These syncopated row stripes are repeated twice more, then one more brioche knit stripe is worked. The stitches are then divided over two needles and each set of stitches is worked in a 1x1 ribbing to create the first keyhole. The stitches are then placed back onto one needle and the neck wrap section is worked. When that section is long enough, the stitches will once again be divided and worked as the second ribbed keyhole. The scarf is finished by working the second tail.

Hang a marker on the right side (RS) of the work.

The first edge stitch of every brioche row is a "sl1 wyib". After slipping this stitch, pull the yarn tight.

INSTRUCTIONS

CO 20 sts.

Set-Up Row WS: sl1 wyib, *k1, sl1yo; rep from * to last st, k1.
Work BRIOCHE KNIT STRIPE.

BRIOCHE KNIT STRIPE
Brioche Knit Row: sl1 wyib, *brk1, sl1yo; rep from * to last st, k1.

Rep **Brioche Knit Row**, 7 more times ending with a WS row. (you can count 4 yo's going up the inside of a purl column - see Figure 1) Remember that two worked rows = one counted row in a column of stitches. Hang a marker on the RS.

Figure 1 - count 4 yarn overs up the inside of a purl column on the RS. That means you have worked 8 rows.

Switch to working BRIOCHE PURL STRIPE.

BRIOCHE PURL STRIPE
Brioche Purl Row: sl1 wyib, yf, *brp1, sl1yo; rep from * to last st, k1.

Rep **Brioche Purl Row**, 7 more times.

Work **Brioche Knit Row** 8 times.
Work **Brioche Purl Row** 8 times.
Work **Brioche Knit Row** 8 times.

FIRST KEYHOLE
With RS facing, separate the stitches onto two needles. Place first st on thin circular needle and hold to the back, place second st on a second thin circular needle and hold to the front, third st on back needle, 4th stitch on front needle. See Figure 2.

Figure 2 - place first st on thin circular needle and hold to the back, place second st on second thin circular needle and hold to the front.

Continue dividing the stitches, alternating between the back and front needles, until you have 10 stitches on the front needle and 10 stitches on the back needle. See Figure 3.

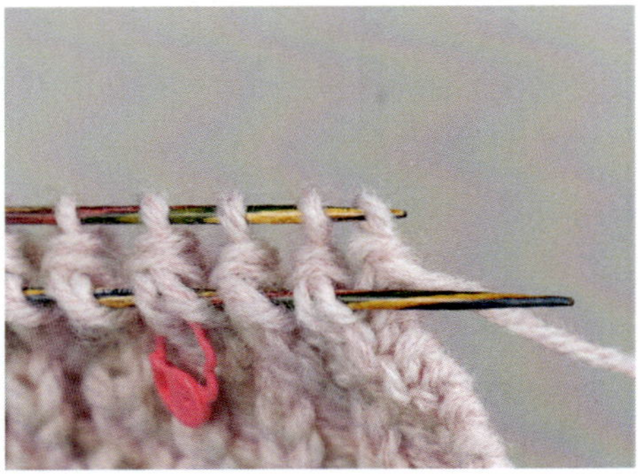

Figure 3 - the stitches are divided onto smaller circular needles. Begin the keyhole by working the front set of stitches off of the smaller needle onto the size 7 (4.5 mm) needle.

Do not cut yarn. With RS facing, work the stitches on the front needle. For this first row, you can work off of the small circular needle onto the size 7 (4.5 mm) needle: *brk1, brp1; rep from * to last 2 sts, brk1, p1.

Front Keyhole Row: *k1, p1; rep from *.

Rep **Front Keyhole Row**, 10 more times ending with a WS row. Cut the yarn. Transfer the Front Keyhole stitches to a smaller circular needle and the Back Keyhole stitches to the working size 7 (4.5 mm) needle. Work the back keyhole starting on the RS which is the inside of the keyhole.

Back Keyhole Row: *p1, k1; rep from *.

Rep **Back Keyhole Row**, 11 more times ending with a WS row.

With RS facing, place sts, alternately, back onto a small circular needle, beginning with a back keyhole stitch. See Figure 4.

Figure 4 - after working front and back keyholes, with RS facing, place sts, alternately, back onto a small circular needle.

Work off of the small circular needle onto the working size 7 (4.5 mm) needle. See Figure 5. Begin the NECK WRAP.

Figure 5 - work off of the small circular needle onto the size 7 (4.5 mm) needle for the Neck Wrap.

NECK WRAP

Set-Up Row RS: p1, *k1, sl1yo; rep from *to last st, k1.

Brioche Knit Row: sl1 wyib, *brk1, sl1yo; rep from * to last st, k1.

Rep the **Brioche Knit Row** until Neck Wrap is 17.5" (44cm) long or desired length that fits comfortably around your neck. End with a WS row.

SECOND KEYHOLE

Divide the stitches as before and work as for FIRST KEYHOLE. After working the second keyhole and placing stitches, alternately, back onto one working needle, with RS facing, begin the SECOND TAIL.

SECOND TAIL

Set-Up Row RS: sl1 wyib, *k1, sl1yo; rep from * to last st, k1.

BRIOCHE KNIT STRIPE

Brioche Knit Row: sl1 wyib, *brk1, sl1yo; rep from * to last st, k1.

Rep **Brioche Knit Row**, 6 more times.

Switch to working BRIOCHE PURL STRIPES.

BRIOCHE PURL STRIPE

Brioche Purl Row: sl1 wyib, *brp1, sl1yo; rep from * to last st, k1.

Rep **Brioche Purl Row**, 7 more times.

Work **Brioche Knit Row** 8 times.
Work **Brioche Purl Row** 8 times.
Work **Brioche Knit Row** 8 times.

Bind off. Weave in ends. I did not block the scarf.

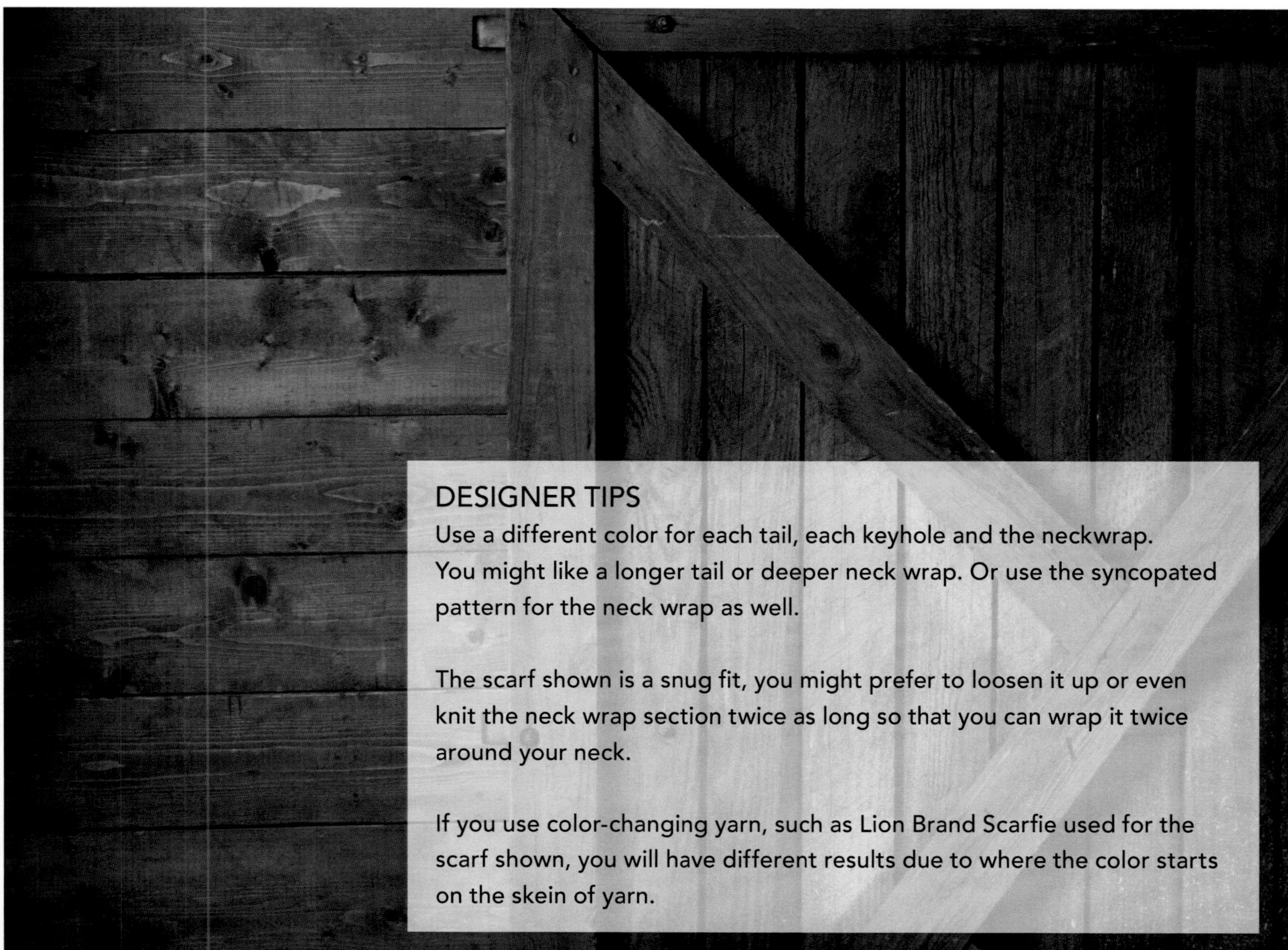

DESIGNER TIPS

Use a different color for each tail, each keyhole and the neckwrap. You might like a longer tail or deeper neck wrap. Or use the syncopated pattern for the neck wrap as well.

The scarf shown is a snug fit, you might prefer to loosen it up or even knit the neck wrap section twice as long so that you can wrap it twice around your neck.

If you use color-changing yarn, such as Lion Brand Scarfie used for the scarf shown, you will have different results due to where the color starts on the skein of yarn.

Classic Brioche Cowl

SHOPPING LIST

(Medium Weight) 4 MEDIUM
[3.5 ounces, 210 yards
(100 grams, 192 meters) per skein]:
- ☐ Pumpkin (CC) - 2 skeins
- ☐ Beige (MC) - 2 skeins

KNITTING NEEDLES

24" (61 cm) Circular
- ☐ Size 7 (4.5 mm) or size needed for gauge

ADDITIONAL SUPPLIES

- ☐ Stitch marker

FINISHED SIZE

11½" high x 56" circumference (29 cm x 142 cm)

GAUGE

In brioche stitch, 13 sts and 19 counted rows/rnds = 4" (10 cm)

TECHNIQUES USED

- brk, sl1yo *(See pages 8 and 9)*
- brp1, sl1yo *(See page 10)*
- Two-Color Brioche in the Round *(See page 12)*

INTERMEDIATE

PATTERN NOTES

Hang marker on needle between the last and first stitch of the round.

INSTRUCTIONS

With Pumpkin, CO 182 sts. Join for working in the round making sure the CO is not twisted. Hang marker.

Set-Up Round 1: with Pumpkin, knit.
Set-Up Round 2: with Pumpkin, purl.
Set-Up Round 3: with Beige, *k1, sl1yo; rep from *.
Set-Up Round 4: with Pumpkin, *sl1yo, brp1; rep from *.

Round 1: with Beige, *brk1, sl1yo; rep from *.
Round 2: with Pumpkin, *sl1yo, brp1; rep from *.

Repeat **Round 1** and **Round 2** until cowl measures 11¼" (28.5 cm) or desired height.

Work **Round 1** one more time, cut Beige.

Finishing Round 1: with Pumpkin, *brk1, k1: rep from *.
Finishing Round 2: with Pumpkin, purl.

Bind off in knit with Pumpkin.

DESIGNER TIPS

This cowl would also look good with a smaller circumference so that it sits close to the neck.

You can change colors as you go, work the brp rounds in various stripes of color. Or make color stripes in the brk and brp rounds.

Brioche Hat

SHOPPING LIST

YARN
(Light Weight) 3 LIGHT
[3.5 ounces, 306 yards
(5100 grams, 280 meters) per skein]:
- ☐ Beige (MC) - 1 skein
- ☐ Pink (CC) - 1 skein

KNITTING NEEDLES
16" (40.5 cm) Circular
- ☐ Size 5 (3.75 mm) or size needed for gauge

Double Pointed (set of 4)
- ☐ Size 5 (3.75 mm) (for crown)

ADDITIONAL SUPPLIES
- ☐ Stitch marker
- ☐ Tapestry needle
- ☐ Pompom

9¾" high x 17½" circumference (25 cm x 44.5 cm) at ribbing, unstretched

GAUGE
In brioche stitch, 20 sts and 26 counted rounds = 4" (10 cm)

TECHNIQUES USED
- brk, sl1yo *(See pages 8 and 9)*
- brp1, sl1yo *(See page 10)*
- Two-Color Brioche in the Round *(See page 12)*
- brLsl dec *(See page 13)*

INTERMEDIATE

DESIGNER TIPS

You could make you own pompom. Try making one from left over yarns using different types of yarns and colors.

This hat could be made in only one color. Just follow the instructions as if you were using the two colors. That means that you will end the brk round with a sl1yo, slip the marker, and start the brp round with a sl1yo in the same yarn. Then when you finish a brp round with a brp1, slip the marker, work the first stitch of a brk round; brk1.

PATTERN NOTES

Hang marker on needle between the last and first stitch of the round.

INSTRUCTIONS

With MC, CO 108 sts. Join for working in the round making sure the CO is not twisted. Hang marker.

RIBBING

Round 1: with Beige, *k1, p1; rep from *.

Rep **Round 1**, 17 more times.

BRIOCHE HAT BODY

Set-Up Round 1: with Beige, *k1, sl1yo; rep from *.
Set-Up Round 2: with Pink, *sl1yo, brp1; rep from *.

Round 1: with Beige, *brk1, sl1yo; rep from *.
Round 2: with Pink, *sl1yo, brp1; rep from *.

Repeat **Rounds 1 and 2** until total height is 8" (20.5 cm) or desired height. Note that the following crown section adds 1¾" (4.5 cm).

CROWN SECTION

Change to double pointed needles (dividing evenly among 3 needles) when there are too few stitches for circular needle.
Round 1: with Beige, *brLsl dec, sl1yo, (brk1, sl1yo) 7 times, pm; rep from *. You should have 6 decreases evenly placed around the crown. 96 sts.
Round 2: with Pink, *sl1yo, brp1; rep from *.

Round 3: with Beige, *brLsl dec, sl1yo, work (brk1, sl1yo) to marker, sm; rep from *. 84 sts.
Round 4: as **Round 2.**

Rep **Rounds 3 and 4** 6 times: 12 sts. Cut both yarns about 12" (30.5 cm) long. With a tapestry needle, run yarns through the remaining 12 stitches twice. Pull tightly to close and secure ends.

Weave in ends. Attach pompom.

Finishing and General Instructions

Correcting a dropped yarn over

The most common mistake in brioche knitting is a dropped yarn over. This creates a annoying little horizontal bar that just glares out at you that needs to be repaired.

The best way to repair this dropped yarn over is to unravel the column, fix your mistake and then chain the stitches back up the column. Do this very carefully, trying to keep the "stitch" in front and it's "yarn over" hanging to the back.

Here is a tried and true method for repairing a dropped yarn over. Please, don't do this at the end of the evening. Wait until you can patiently make this repair

Work up to the knit column with the dropped yarn over that needs to be repaired.

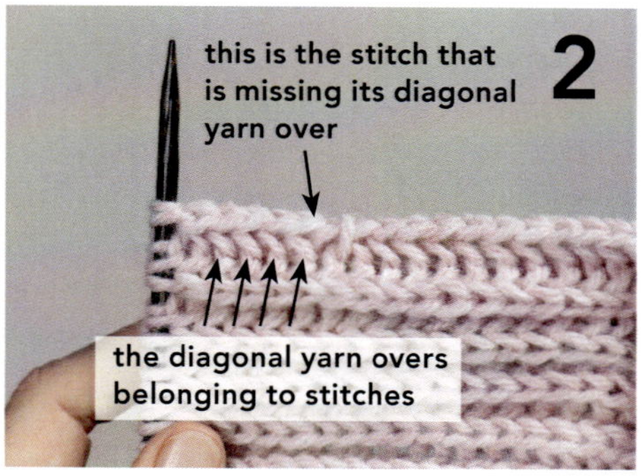

Fold the fabric along the knit column to see where the dropped yarn over needs to be restored.

Hang a marker in the space where the dropped yarn over will need to be hung.

Drop the stitch from the needle,

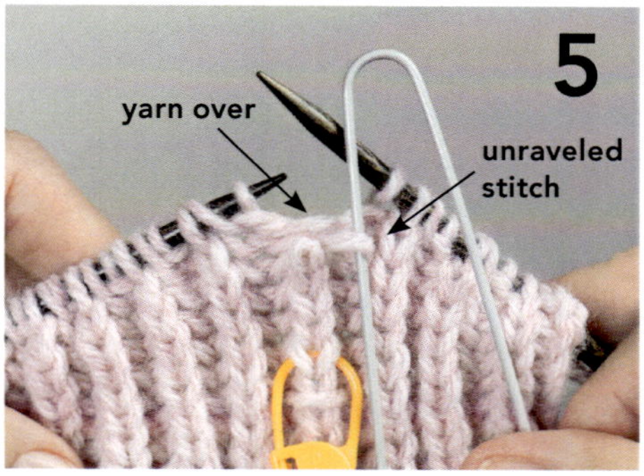

unravel and place the stitch only, leaving yo behind, on a stitch holder. Continue popping off the stitches,

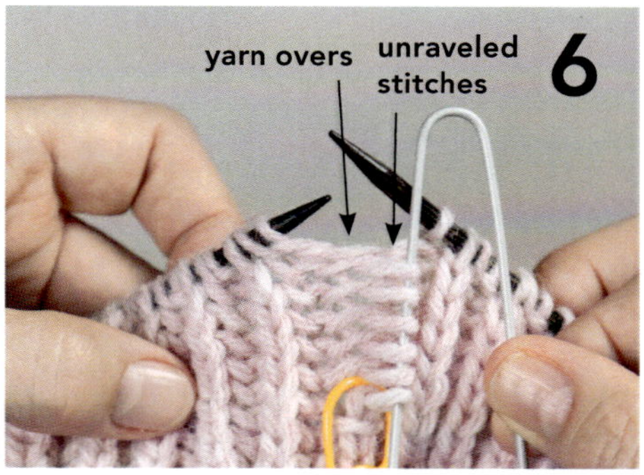

placing them on the stitch holder, leaving their yarn overs hanging underneath, until you reach the marker.

Remove the marker, pull up the dropped yarn over and lay it behind its designated stitch.

Now chain up the stitches caught on the stitch holder until you reach the top stitch. Don't remove from stitch holder until all stitches have been chained.

After all the stitches have been chained, remove the stitch holder, and place the final stitch together with its yarn over onto the needle.

Conventional K1, P1 Bind Off

When working the conventional k1, p1 bind off, directly after finishing a brioche row, use a larger needle than that used to knit the piece. That way, the bind off isn't too tight.

This sample shown starts with a one stitch selvedge edge that is slipped wyib at the beginning of every row and ends with a k1.

With yarn in back, slip the first stitch,

**brk1,*

pass the first stitch over,

purl the following stitch,

*pass the first stitch over. Repeat from * to last stitch. End with k1, pass first stitch over.*

The finished conventional k1, p1, bind off.

Stem Stitch Bind Off

This leaves a bind off with an appearance similar to the 2-color long tail cast on.

Cut yarn at least 3 times as long as the top edge of your project and thread it onto a tapestry needle.

I find that after working 10 or so stitches, I generally have to go back and pull up and tighten them.

**Insert the needle into the second stitch from front to back and pull the yarn through.*

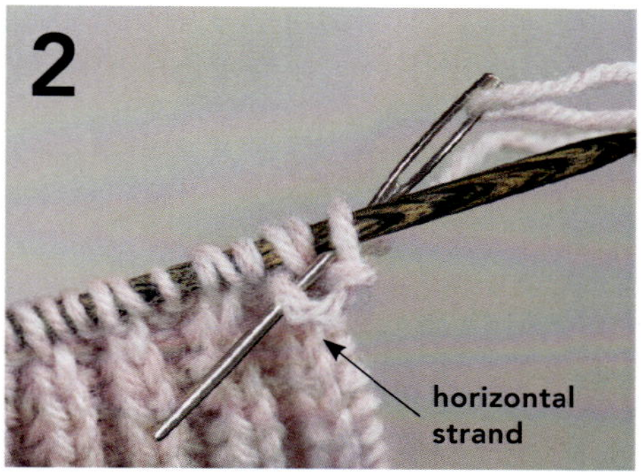

Then insert needle into the first stitch from back to front, going under the horizontal strand just made.

*Pull the yarn through and drop the first stitch from the knitting needle. Repeat from *. You see the needle is now inserted into the second stitch...*

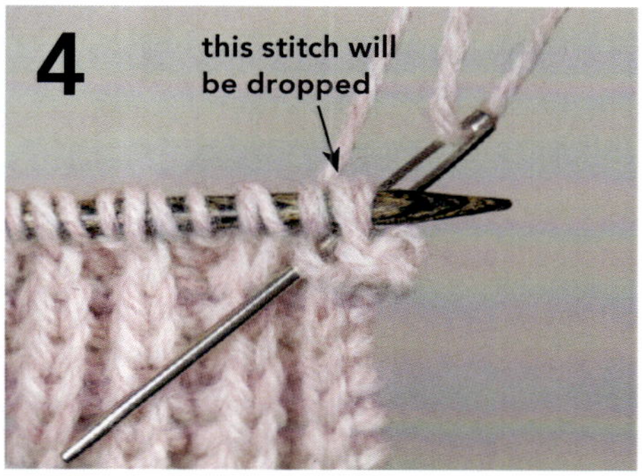

... and then the first stitch from back to front, going under the horizontal strand just made.

This bind off can also be loosened or tightened after it is worked.

Weaving in Ends

The brioche stitch creates nice little pockets to hide yarn ends.

Thread the end onto a tapestry needle, then weave the ends between the yarn overs as shown. Try and "catch" a bit of the yarn over thread with your tapestry needle to help keep the end from slipping out.

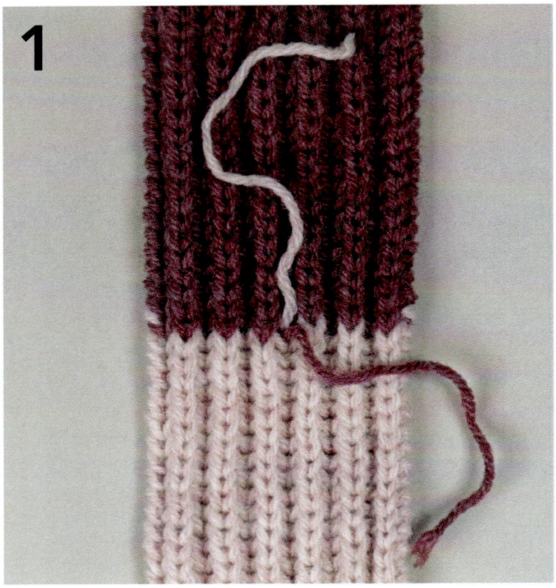

The example above has 2 ends that need to be sewn in.

Thread a yarn end onto a tapestry needle and sew up between yarn overs on the inside of a purl column. Pull through.

For the second yarn end, carry it behind one stitch then sew in the same manner as with the first yarn end. Pull through.

Clip yarns.

Blocking

Brioche is stretchy but not elastic. If it stretches out, it will not bounce back to its original shape so block pieces cautiously.

Blocking is used to relax your stitches. If you want your brioche fabric to be cushy (this depends upon the material as well) then don't block it.

However, if you want the piece slightly relaxed then steam block it lightly. Sometimes the selvedge edges can be a bit flared. If this happens, lightly steam block it. Straighten it while it is damp, and let it dry.

STEAM BLOCKING

Spread a thin damp cloth over the wrong side of the knitted piece and very gently touch the iron to the damp cloth, creating lots of steam. This will relax the yarn and ease the piece into shape. Don't press down and flatten the knitting.

Hot irons will melt certain fibers such as acrylic, polyester, and nylon so use heat with caution. I lightly steam blocked most of the projects shown in this book.

WET BLOCKING AND WASHING

When wet blocking or washing a brioche piece, stretching can become a problem because of the weight of the absorbed water.

To counteract this, when washing or wet blocking, squeeze out as much water as you can while supporting the piece. Wrap it in a thick dry towel, then several layers of newspaper, and tread on it to get out as much water as possible without stretching the piece. Then ease the piece back into its original shape and dry it flat.

Knitting Abbreviations

g = grams
in = inches
cm = centimeters
m = meters
mm = millimeters
yd = yards

BO = bind off
brk = brioche knit
brLsl dec = brioche left slant decrease
brp = brioche purl
CC = contrast color
CO = cast on
k = knit
MC = main color
p = purl
pm = place marker
rep = repeat
rnd(s) = round(s)
RS = right (public) side of work
sl1 = slip 1 (purlwise, unless told otherwise)
sl1 wyib = slip 1 purlwise with yarn in back
sl1yo = slip stitch with a yarn over
sm = slip marker
st(s) = stitch(es)
tog = together
WS = wrong side of work
wyib = with yarn in back
wyif = with yarn in front
yb = take yarn to back under the needle
yf = bring yarn to the front under the needle
yo = yarn over

* = work instructions following * as many more times as indicated in addition to the first time
( ) or [ ] = work enclosed instructions as many times as specified by the number immediately following or contains explanatory remarks.

KNIT TERMINOLOGY		
UNITED STATES		**INTERNATIONAL**
gauge	=	tension
bind off	=	cast off
yarn over (YO)	=	yarn forward (yfwd) **or** yarn around needle (yrn)

KNITTING NEEDLES																			
U.S.	0	1	2	3	4	5	6	7	8	9	10	10½	11	13	15	17	19	35	50
U.K.	13	12	11	10	9	8	7	6	5	4	3	2	1	00	000	---	---	---	---
Metric - mm	2	2.25	2.75	3.25	3.5	3.75	4	4.5	5	5.5	6	6.5	8	9	10	12.75	15	19	25

BASIC	Projects using basic stitches. May include basic increases and decreases.
EASY	Projects may include simple stitch patterns, color work, and/or shaping.
INTERMEDIATE	Projects may include involved stitch patterns, color work, and/or shaping.
COMPLEX	Projects may include complex stitch patterns, color work, and/or shaping using a variety of techniques and stitches simultaneously.

Yarn Weight Symbol & Names	SUPER FINE 1	FINE 2	LIGHT 3	MEDIUM 4	BULKY 5	SUPER BULKY 6	JUMBO 7
Type of Yarns in Category	Sock, Fingering, Baby	Sport, Baby	DK, Light Worsted	Worsted, Afghan, Aran	Chunky, Craft, Rug	Bulky, Roving	Jumbo, Roving

* GUIDELINES ONLY: The chart above reflects the most commonly used gauges and needle sizes for specific yarn categories.

** Lace weight yarns are usually knitted on larger needles to create lacy openwork patterns.
Accordingly, a gauge range is difficult to determine. Always follow the gauge stated in your pattern.

Yarn Information

Projects in this book were made using various weights of yarn. Any brand of the specified weight of yarn may be used. It is best to refer to the yardage/meters when determining how many balls or skeins to purchase. Remember, to arrive at the finished size, it is the GAUGE/TENSION that is important, not the brand of yarn.

CLASSIC BRIOCHE SCARF

Red Heart® Chic Sheep by Marly Bird™
#5632 Polo

BULKY BRIOCHE SCARF

Lion Brand® Wool-Ease® Thick & Quick® Bonus Bundle®
#525 Wild Strawberry

HEADBAND

Sugar Bush Shiver
#1415 Frost Bite

BRIOCHE GARTER BLOCK SCARF

Patons® Classic Wool Worsted™
#00229 Natural Mix

BRIOCHE COWLETTE

Red Heart® Evermore™
#9933 Cotton Candy
#9935 Mulberry
#9936 Autumn

PONCHO

Lion Brand® Wool-Ease® (Colors are named from lightest to darkest color)
Beige #98 Natural Heather
Blush Pink #104 Blush Heather
Rose Pink #140 Rose Heather
Light Grey #151 Grey Heather
Dark Grey #152 Oxford Grey

KEYHOLE SCARF

Lion Brand® Scarfie®
#216 Cream/Silver

CLASSIC BRIOCHE COWL

Patons® Classic Wool Worsted™
#77605 Pumpkin
#00229 Natural Mix

BRIOCHE HAT

Lion Brand Collection® Superwash Merino
Beige #123 Hemp
Pink #139 Peony

Pompom
Bernat® Faux Fur Pompom
#01013 Brown Muskrat

Projects made by Nancy Marchant, Mieka John, Hinke Schreuders and Daan Vromans.
Portrait Photo–Alexandra Feo; How To Photos–Rob van Dijck

Library of Congress Control Number: 2019945789

Made in U.S.A.